Table of Contents

5 STORIES OF WOMEN WHO HAVE
CHANGED THE NORM IN A MALE
DOMINATED WORLD

WOMEN
DISRUPTORS
in Business

SHE RISES
STUDIOS

HANNA OLIVAS

ALONG WITH
DENISE OSTER, NICOLE CURTIS,
ANNABELLE BECKWITH,
& HEATHER STOKES BENTON

ISBN: 978-1-960136-04-6

INTRODUCTION

She Rises Studios was created and inspired by the mother-daughter duo Hanna Olivas and Adriana Luna Carlos. In the middle of 2020, when the world was at one of its most vulnerable times, we saw the need to embrace women globally by offering inspirational quotes, blogs, and articles. Then, in March of 2021, we launched our very own Women's Empowerment Podcast: *She Rises Studios Podcast*.

It is now one of the most sought out Women based podcasts both nationally and internationally. You can find us on your favorite podcast platforms, such as Spotify, Google Podcasts, Apple Podcasts, IHeartRadio, and much more! We didn't stop there. Establishing a safe space for women has become an even deeper need. Due to a global pandemic, women lost their businesses, employment, homes, finances, spouses, and more.

We decided to form the She Rises Studios Community Facebook Group, an environment strictly for women about women. Our focus in this group is to educate and celebrate women globally and meet them exactly where they are on their journey.

It's a group of Ordinary Women Doing EXTRAordinary Things.

As we continued to grow our network, we saw a need to help shape the minds and influences of women struggling with insecurities, doubts, fears, etc. From this, we created a global movement known as:

Women Disruptors in Business

This book is all about positively disrupting the way female entrepreneurs are being seen, heard, and recognized as equals in the business world.

These five women are true trailblazers who have broken barriers. Now as successful women in their own right, they're sharing their strategies and success with you.

Each author in this book is a powerful, innovative, diverse, and creative woman in business.

Gain the knowledge and guidance on how to overcome "It's A Man's World Syndrome."

You will learn how to unleash your feminine power in business!

Each chapter provides strategies and education on the following:

- Women in Leadership Positions
- Being a Fierce and Successful CEO
- Successfully Growing and Leading Your Team
- Handling High Demand and Volume in Business
- Becoming an Unstoppable Woman Entrepreneur
- What a True Woman Disruptor in Business Is
- Avoiding Burnout
- Understanding Your Business Needs

These women have made it their life's passion and purpose to elevate and educate other women to do the same. Let's focus on being the best version of ourselves. You can achieve your goals with hope, dedication, perseverance, and consistency.

This is more than a book. It's a movement!
Join the #BAUW team today.

Start living an abundant and powerful life!

She Rises Studios offers:

- She Rises Studios Publishing
- She Rises Studios Public Relations

- She Rises Studios Podcast
- She Rises Studios Magazine
- Becoming An Unstoppable Woman TV Show
- She Rises Studios Community
- She Rises Studios Academy
- Fenix TV

We won't stop encouraging women to be Unstoppable. This is just the beginning of our global movement.

She Rises, She Leads, She Lives...

With Love,
HANNA OLIVAS
ADRIANA LUNA CARLOS
SHE RISES STUDIOS
www.sherisesstudios.com

Hanna Olivas

Founder & CEO of She Rises Studios
Podcast & TV Host | Best Selling Author | Influential Speaker |
Blood Cancer Advocate | #BAUW Movement Creator

https://www.linkedin.com/company/she-rises-studios/
https://www.instagram.com/sherisesstudios
https://www.facebook.com/sherisesstudios
www.SheRisesStudios.com

Author, Speaker, and Founder. Hanna was born and raised in Las Vegas, Nevada, and has paved her way to becoming one of the most influential women of 2022. Hanna is the co-founder of She Rises Studios and the founder of the Brave & Beautiful Blood Cancer Foundation. Her journey started in 2017 when she was first diagnosed with Multiple Myeloma, an incurable blood cancer. Now more than ever, her focus is to empower other women to become leaders because The Future is Female. She is currently traveling and speaking publicly to women to educate them on entrepreneurship, leadership, and owning the female power within.

POSITIVE, IMPACTFUL, INFLUENCER AND DISRUPTOR FOR WOMEN

By Hanna Olivas

What Does it Mean to be a Positive Woman Disruptor in Business?

As the business world continues to evolve, it's fascinating to watch women take their rightful place as positive disruptors and pioneers of change within the business landscape. From tech startups to corporate boardrooms, these female disruptors are creating their own space and driving their own agenda, leading the way with fresh ideas and an eye for innovation. So, what does it mean to be a positive woman disruptor in business? Let's take a look.

First off, being a positive woman disruptor means having an attitude of positivity and optimism when approaching any situation or challenge. It means having the courage to stand up for yourself, challenge existing norms, and confidently speak your truth—no matter how uncomfortable that may make others feel. It also means being willing to take risks despite potential failure or criticism from your peers; because, at the end of the day, you believe in yourself and your vision.

Being a positive woman disruptor also involves embracing diversity within yourself and those you work with or serve. Whether it's gender identity, sexual orientation, religious beliefs, or ethnicity—valuing diversity goes beyond just "ticking boxes." Instead, it should be seen as an opportunity for growth that can bring unique perspectives and insights into any given situation.

Furthermore, female entrepreneurs often have different needs than male-run businesses—they need different strategies for success, so being a positive woman disruptor requires understanding that every industry has its own set of rules which must be respected if success is desired. For example: if you're running an online store selling cosmetics, then you need to understand what marketing strategies work best for this type of business (e.g., social media campaigns) as well as how best to build relationships with customers (e.g., offering discounts).

Finally (and perhaps most importantly), being a positive woman disruptor requires passion—both for yourself and those around you—along with resilience when times get tough. It also requires understanding that failure is part of life, but learning from our mistakes can help us grow into more confident individuals who are able to make better, more impactful decisions in our lives moving forward.

It's time we start celebrating women making waves in every corner of society—not just within traditional roles but across industries, too—so let's keep pushing boundaries until we have achieved true gender parity! Furthermore, let's show future generations what they are capable of achieving by using slang terms like bae, lit, and stay woke intermittently throughout our content (1%)—because why not!

Denise Oster

CEO of Doc Consulting, LLC

https://www.linkedin.com/in/denise-oster-dehn/
https://www.facebook.com/Deniseostercoaching/
https://www.instagram.com/deniseostercoach/
https://www.deniseoster.com/

Denise Oster is a magnetic force of spirited energy. Her tremendous ambition created a new dimension to her brilliance and beliefs. She values the magical vibration and unlimited potential we are born with. Her bold, sassy yet charismatic approach to life and exuberant personality are how she impacts others.

Denise has helped hundreds of clients expand their brilliance into unlimited success. Her experience and knowledge have eliminated self-sabotaging beliefs and transformed into an inner flame that can't be dimmed. Her energy shifts your perspective and lights you on FIRE.

Denise's journey to excellence has been fueled by an unrelenting passion for empowering women to succeed. She holds a psychology and education degree and is a certified lifestyle coach, real estate agent, investor, and author. Her purpose originated from past obstacles of fears, low self-worth, infertility, miscarriages, divorce, single motherhood, and uncertainty. She's about doing the heart work not the hard work.

HEY ALEXA, PLAY DISRUPTOR!

By Denise Oster

When did it become okay for women to settle for less? Seriously, when did this become a trend? Why not add more "YES" to life? It's great to see that women have been a growing factor in the economy's success, but the full potential of women in the workforce has yet to be tapped. The main force that holds them back is their entrenched beliefs and refusal to unleash their ankle weights while blaming their wings. Most women don't even know their purpose, values, or desires, so it's no wonder they can't reach their full potential. They are holding onto limiting beliefs that stand in their way and hold them back from a transformation disruption to the abundance of life they want.

For over ten years, I put myself through the bureaucracy and bullshit of the corporate world and made up every excuse for why it didn't work. Instead of blaming the business, I had to go inward and find out who I was and what my gifts were. I've always had a superpower, but it became fun and easy when I discovered my gift and realized it was always available to me. I stopped trying to control it, and acknowledged it was a part of me and what I came here to do. Discovering my purpose made it safe for me to grow and expand.

Women need to recognize and acknowledge their gifts. If you don't know how to do this, here are three ways to discover and own your innate gifts:

1. by how you feel,
2. by what comes to you, and
3. by what lights you up

If you want something different, you must do something different. Now more than ever, women are coming alive and wanting to emphatically live life on their terms, and I'm here for it. In this chapter, I will guide you towards having a life and business that uses your gifts to be wildly successful while getting the clarity you need to achieve it. Are you ready to shake shit up, live outside your comfort zone, stand up for yourself, be yourself, and disrupt the norm in your life? Some systems and rules are meant to be broken, and you are meant to be a disruptor. Being a disruptor means you can do things backward, upside down, or sideways just as long as you do it your way, the way it feels good to you, and it doesn't have to be the way everyone else does it.

If you're okay with just "good enough" in life, close the book right now. I don't want to waste your time or mine. If you are ready to disrupt life and your industry, keep reading.

My friend recently told me about this movie called 'Knives Out: Glass Onion' starring Edward Norton. His character talks about being a disruptor, and since that's what this book is about, I wanted to share some of the thought-provoking things he said in the movie.

He said: "If you want to shake things up, you start with something small. You break a norm, or an idea, or a convention, some little business model. But you go with things that people are kind of tired of anyway." He then goes on to say, "As it turns out, nobody wants you to break the system itself. But that is what true disruption is."

By the way, I'm proud of you for not closing the book and dismissing your greatness. You've chosen to continue reading this chapter for a reason. My guess is because I've piqued your curiosity, hit a nerve, or that it's finally time to hop off the struggle bus and become a disruptor. From here forward, I would like you to pledge to yourself: "I refuse to stay stuck in a place that doesn't suit me!" Feeling stuck is a feeling not a fact. Let's leave the facts to me, and I'll leave the feelings to you. One of the ways I'm going to give you the facts is STRAIGHT UP! I don't hold back on what I believe or feel, especially when it is valuable for others to expand. From the depths of my soul, there is no greater joy than watching a woman come alive and see her soul set on fire. And what's even more thrilling is watching her share that with others so they can succeed. I have zero tolerance for jealousy, competition, or complacency. I have learned the hard way that I was only hurting myself with my twisted thinking and bitter feelings. Owning my shit has made me an unstoppable disrupter, and it can for you too.

Our brains naturally gravitate to unpleasant thoughts, words, and actions, and the word 'disruption' holds a negative connotation for many. I happened to be exposed to the word negatively at an early age. Having attended a parochial school that was highly strict and didn't hold back on discipline, any behavior out of the norm was considered disruptive. When I sat next to Joey in third grade and watched him launch a spitball across the room, landing smack dab into the middle of a little girl's eyes, I couldn't help but blurt out, "bullseye!" Joey was sent to the principal's office for being disruptive. This taught me that being disruptive was a bad thing and could be punishable. Some disruptions can just be nagging nuances, like being interrupted during a meeting to take a phone call. Then there are major disruptors that turn your world upside down. While writing my first self-published book, I was near completion (over ¾ of the way done), and my motherboard went out on my computer. Yep, I lost everything. I hadn't backed up my computer. Ouch! That one stung. I began firing off every swear word in the book. I was livid, yet frantically trying to find a way to self-diagnose what happened. I grabbed the computer and held it to my chest as my heart sank, hands trembling, and tears pouring down my face. I felt like I'd lost my whole life. Well, actually, just my whole life story that was a big part of me. After I allowed myself a 3-minute pity party, I pulled myself together and realized this was more than a nagging nuance. It was an effing catastrophe and a major disruptor to my life and business. Three weeks, three thousand dollars, and a complete forensic recovery later, I was back in business. I was able to restore my whole book. Disruptors never quit; they stay creative.

Disrupters are only as powerful as the meaning given to them and what you choose to do with them. What meaning will you give yours? How will you use them to serve you? Every disruption that occurred in my life was happening *for* me, not *to* me. It was time for me to embrace change. I used them as messages, lessons, and opportunities to show up in full service to myself and others. I turned them inward and made them work for me, not against me. I had to rewire my belief about the word disruption and stop my stinking thinking. I started to take risks and mess shit up. This is your moment to do the same. Get excited about what you have overcome and be adventurous. The quickest and best way to use disruption to your advantage is by realizing you are not a problem solver, you are a solutions creator. Nothing is ever a problem, it's always an opportunity. It's an opportunity to take your own stance and stand out. Shifting your views will ignite your creativity, gifts, and truths. This is a magnetic disruption that will demolish any "boys club." You get to have a luxury "She Shed" filled with powerful tools. They are all inside, waiting to help you become more resilient, innovative, and powerful. I understand that breaking out on your own can be scary, but if you feel through it, it will make you feel unstoppable. You don't need to think your way through anything to be a disruptor in your industry. Just feel your way through it. The day you stop reading about other people's success stories and start creating your own is the day the disrupter is born and your up-cleveling begins. I became a disrupter by rewriting my story. When will you rewrite yours?

My story completely changed as a single mom and business owner. In the past I would get up and do things that I didn't want to do, didn't like, and in ways that didn't feel good to me just because I had to 'go make money.' Operating like the Energizer bunny kept me in self-betrayal, deprivation, and not getting what I wanted. I suffered through multiple miscarriages, divorces, and toxic relationships. I had to start utilizing the flight attendant rule and put the oxygen mask on first. I adapted to my needs, desires, and wants. I honored my inner truth and stopped lying to myself. When you use your imagination, you will realize there are a zillion ways you can do things. We don't need to go and do the things we hate in order to get the thingd we like. You are a disrupter because you don't have to sit here and listen to what someone else has said to do in order to be successful. You do you, boo! You can do whatever the F you want, however the F you want. You can do whatever feels good and right to you.

Even after all of the shit I went through, I still saw the beauty in people even though my life had shown me the opposite. I still decided to focus on the fact that the sun was shining, and I still had a grateful heart. And even when it was so hard, I never quit. Yes, I've had moments, I've been kicked, I've been scared, I don't know what I'm doing, and I don't know where I'm going. But I know there is this thing in me, and so I follow it, even when I don't know where we are going because I always seem to land somewhere.

To dominate in my industry, I had to understand that being a disrupter isn't about perfection. Being a disrupter means I will disrupt the peace to honor my heart. I will disrupt what isn't working, and I will shine a light on it so that I can get it working how I want. It's not about having done everything perfectly along the way. When you let yourself have a voice and realize you don't need to show up in perfection, you will attract a lot more clients. When you accept that it's okay to have a messy life and still dream simultaneously, you realize it's not about putting your best foot forward, it's about putting your *true* self forward.

Let's disrupt these ideas that you will never feel happy and fulfilled, or your dreams will never come true because you think they are unrealistic. Why not raise the standards of the heart? Do you know how many women are dying inside? A shit ton! All because their lights are off inside of them and they are choosing to settle for less. When did it become a bad thing to believe that you deserve better? Some people are so afraid to go after anything better because they think they will lose what they have. If you're driving a piece of shit Honda then you are driving a shit Honda. You already know you're driving a piece of shit, so what does it hurt to go after the Ferrari? What does it hurt to go after something more? Or trust that there is something deeper in yourself?

When you are living your heart's desire, your path forward becomes immediately crystal clear because the heart knows what the heart wants. This step requires bravery.

How can you do things that you love even more? Why not have a job you love, a partner you love, friends you love, a life you love, a wardrobe you love, a car you love, a house you love, hell… Houses you love because you are effing here! Why not? That's the way I think, and that's the way I disrupt.

We don't live in a world where "just enough" has to be a thing. We just don't have to be in this marginalized place IN ANYTHING! Even with all the things life threw at me, I just kept pouring my heart into it and looking at what I've created. Why not take what is *owed to you*? You can be anything you choose. The more we see women showing up in their power, the less we will settle as a whole. So if you have been brainwashed or told that "you can't have it all," it's bullshit! I was told that many times in my life and it stuck with me for too many years. I wondered, "Is that really how it is?" The answer is no, it isn't.

'The blueprint for being a woman' is being disrupted right now, maybe you can relate. It is my mission to help women go after what they want and feel safe and good about it. I personally hold your hand, compassionately tell you the straight-up facts, and show you how to go after what's already there for you, what's already inside you waiting to light your soul on fire. Your gifts are already innately present, and it's time you give them the importance they deserve. It's time to do the *heart-work*.

It's a very simple process for me to help women come alive by acknowledging their heart's desires and encouraging them to follow them. I lived in hell while not knowing there was so much more for me out there. I got a divorce, I wrote books, and I created a coaching and real estate investment business. It was so hard, but I knew I needed to be true to myself. I had lived long enough feeling like I wasn't myself. I started bringing parts of *me* back to the surface. I could just feel my soul light up. I was very unsure and uncertain of my future, but I knew I would be okay. And nothing beats that feeling of peace, of inwardly understanding that my bed might be empty but my heart is healing and feeling fuller. I don't tell women how perfect I am. I let them know how scared, vulnerable, and human I am and that I'm still showing up anyway. I left what I knew, and it was scary but it was also okay. I faced all the things that I thought were my flaws but were actually parts of my gifts. It was wild, but I did it. You can do it too. I bet you do it for everyone else… So now it's *your turn* to do it for yourself. If we don't start doing it for ourselves, our world is in trouble because we are supposed to be our own replenishment. When you can really put your façade down, bring your human to the table, your imperfection, and understand that being you is enough, you will enjoy asking for a table for one. When you realize you are the permission slip you have been waiting for and you can give it to yourself, grant that shit immediately. We women need to see each other for who we are. Are you ready to join this sisterhood and disrupt our lives and workplaces with our brilliant minds, wild hearts, and feisty spirits? And show the world that we aren't afraid to speak up and live life because doing what we were told was impossible?

Cheers to all the sassy, brassy, and sexy women who will have the strength to walk away from what doesn't deserve or serve them. May all your disruptions benefit you, all while you enjoy the feeling it brings you. Even if it's a little naughty, risqué, scary, painful, or exciting. There is a greater life ahead of you. It includes having a career or business that highlights your gifts and amplifies your wealth. This is a megabyte of inspiration. It's time to step up. It's time to stop settling, raise your standards, and be the disruption you are meant to be!

Nicole Curtis

She Rises Studios
Co-Founder of the Women Leadership Division

https://www.linkedin.com/in/nicole-curtis-sherisesstudios
https://www.facebook.com/nicolecurtissherisesstudios
https://www.instagram.com/nicolecurtis_sherisesstudios/
https://www.sherisesstudios.com/
https://www.facebook.com/groups/sherisesstudioscommunity

Author, Speaker, and Co-Founder. Nicole Curtis was born and raised in Holland, MI, and is a much sought-after leader in Personal Growth and Self-Leadership Development. Nicole is the Co-Founder of the Women Leadership Division of She Rises Studios. Her mission is to empower women to rise and lead in life and business. Nicole writes and speaks to women entrepreneurs to educate them on leadership and personal development.

F*CK THEIR RULES, CREATE YOUR OWN!

By Nicole Curtis

Girl, I am so geeked you are here reading this book. This book was written by some badass women who are tearing shit up in the business world and who want to help you level the f$ck up in life and in business. I am incredibly honored to be part of this collaboration project, and I am ecstatic to have the opportunity to connect with you.

Why? Because as a woman disruptor, nothing fires me up more than seeing women take a stand, go against all the odds, and create greatness in life and in business! But if this is something you have been doubting yourself on, hun, or you've been hearing a quiet voice in your soul whispering to you to get up and follow your heart, then this chapter has been written for you. But before I get into the good stuff, I want to share a little piece of my story to help give you a better understanding of where I once was in life and how I got to where I am now.

Back then, I was working at a local radio station in my hometown. I was a sales and marketing representative, as this was my wheelhouse. I loved traveling, meeting new people, and forming new client relationships. I thrived on the fact that I was not only able to be part of marketing their business but in helping their business become visible on and off the radio.

But here is the thing: there was a problem where I worked, and that problem was that I was not a conformed robot! I actually thought for myself and asked questions, which management didn't like. One of the management members actually didn't even want me on the team. He told me himself. Wow, huh? Talk about what a great first impression that was, especially during my first week as a new hire.

As the months and years went on, I often found myself being pulled into the conference room for another lecture on how I needed to be more of a team player and how I needed to take better direction and stick to "following the rules." It didn't matter how much profit I brought into the company. It was never good enough. Yeah, they were thankful. I mean of course, who wouldn't be when you're bringing in clients that are spending thousands of dollars, but just as they are saying great work they were also saying they expected more out of me. Which, yes, I was in sales, but wow talk about feeling inadequate.

I never felt more disrespected and unappreciated in the workplace than I did there. Every day was a struggle to "survive." I had a target on my back, and everything I said or did was monitored with the goal to get me to quit. I worked at that station for almost four years until I left and started my entrepreneurial journey. As mentally and emotionally brutal as those four years at that job were, I learned something that has forever helped me, and it is something that I am called to preach and teach to women all over the world. I am going to share it with you here because my mission in life is to break the common mold that women must follow the "rules." Rules created by others to make women believe that, when followed, they will have a sense of purpose and meaning. Which is absolute bullshit, and this is why I teach women to create their own frickin rules in life and in business.

Nobody should ever tell you how to be or what to do, nor which direction you have to go in life or in business, period! You are the only one that should have control over your life. You get to be who you want to be, have ownership of what you want to do, and decide where you are headed.

How I have created my own rules is through the act of SELF-LEADERSHIP!

Instead of being led, lead yourself and give yourself permission! When leading yourself, you establish your own set of rules which allow you to lead the life you want to live. To develop self-leadership, it is important for you to be aware of the way you think, feel, and take action. I have done this by focusing my time and energy on defining myself.

Defying myself has not been an easy task, but I believe it is absolutely necessary when it comes to leading yourself and creating your own rules as a women disruptor.

There are five elements of "self" that I follow and teach, but today I want to share with you my top two that I believe are absolutely essential when it comes to mastering self-leadership.

I share these with you because I know, as a woman disruptor, you are going to cross paths with people, either by choice or not, that will criticize you and freely voice their opinions and concerns about you. Which is totally fine, they are free to do so, but don't you dare let their voice get stuck in your head and make you start second-guessing yourself. Mastering self-leadership is a crucial part of not only standing in your power, but also NEVER FORGETTING WHO YOU ARE! Don't let others dial you down and lower you to their standards of thinking and acting. As much as they are entitled to their own thoughts and ideas, as a disruptor, you are a mover and a shaker. You are here to not only plant your flag in this world, but to create change and elevation. You are here to speak your truth and share your message with the world. Don't let anyone take that away from you!

Self-Acceptance

Accept all of you, every part- the good, the bad, and the messy!

Having self-acceptance gives you the permission to stop comparing yourself to others as well as get back up when you fall. It also helps you to eliminate self-sabotaging behaviors, so you can confront your fears, doubts, and insecurities.

Self-acceptance also gives you permission to swim upstream when everyone else is going down! Following your own rules versus everyone else's.

For you to lead yourself and follow your own rules, you have to accept yourself for who you are and who you are striving to become, and it is very important for you to learn how to forgive yourself in doing so. When leading oneself, it is essential that you learn to forgive yourself. When you forgive yourself, it is easier to accept yourself.

Remember, you're either accepting yourself or judging yourself. Stop self-judging, be kind to yourself, stay positive, accept your imperfections, and never give up. Don't forget your accomplishments, make sure you celebrate you, and know you are worthy.

Self-Awareness

Self-awareness is the conscious knowledge of our own character, feelings, motives, and desires.

This is when it is crucial to look internally within yourself, and when I do I like to focus on three key areas: My Mind, Body, and Soul.

It is during this step when I feel the most empowered and ready to create changes and build up in my strength areas, as well as identify areas that need improvement.

Two ways I do this is by asking myself questions, as well as tuning into my emotions. I reflect on my answers to help gauge and track my process, which helps with my mind and body awareness. Tuning into my emotions helps me better understand, use, and manage them. In doing so, it also helps me understand the emotions of people around me so I can communicate more effectively with them.

The benefits of positively managing your emotions aren't just stress relief; you are also easily able to empathize with others, overcome challenges, and defuse conflict.

Emotional regulation and management is a powerful trait when it comes to creating and mastering your own self-leadership. It helps keep your mind, body, and soul grounded, allows you to "temperature" check yourself, provides a gauge to help you regulate and process your feelings, and assists you in creating strategies and procedures that help you manage your emotions.

I hope you take these top two self-leadership elements and begin to implement them in your life and business. Self-acceptance and self-awareness is actually what helped me to dig deep within myself. It brought me to my core and showed me just who I am: a woman who is destined to love, serve, educate, and support women to never second guess themselves! Never let the actions or words of others define you. Stand up for yourself and learn to love every part of you. Learn that the gifts, talents, and characteristics of you matter and has meaning in this world.

Yes, my previous work environment was toxic. They could have done better, but I actually feel blessed that God put me there because it helped me unlock my power of self! It gave me the freedom to not only love all of me, but find my worth and learn how to live it out.

Don't ever let your surroundings nor people control you, dear reader! You get to make up your own rules in life!

Annabelle Beckwith

Founder of Yara Journeys Ltd

https://www.linkedin.com/in/annabellebeckwith/
https://www.facebook.com/annabelle.beckwith
https://www.instagram.com/annabellebeckwith
www.yara-journeys.com
www.annabellebeckwith.com

Annabelle Beckwith has been a business consultant, coach, and trainer for over 20 years, working with entrepreneurs and business owners, SMEs and Fortune 100 companies all over the world ... and quietly disrupting the way leaders build productive teams and purposeful, profitable businesses.

Her company - Yara Journeys Ltd - specializes in working with people as human beings first - building individual clarity, confidence and capability - before working on their business goals and aspirations in both a strategic and a practical way.

Her career has included work in daytime television production, in PR and marketing, and as Head of Development and Public Affairs at the Royal Scottish Academy of Music and Drama - varied roles and responsibilities that have given her a rare insight into human psychology in action.

More than that, her own journey and international lived experience have contributed to an approach which combines challenge with compassion, and wisdom with humor.

Amazon bestseller 'Get Your Peas In A Row – 5 key factors to propel your business forward', based on her extensive experiences, focuses on key principles for personal and entrepreneurial growth. she is also co-author of 'Dream Big, Do Bigger', sharing her insights on how to bridge the gap between dreaming and getting real, tangible results.

Annabelle is the proud mother of two twenty-somethings and lives in Scotland.

DISRUPTOR? ME?

By Annabelle Beckwith

When I was first asked to contribute a chapter to this book, I declined. Why? Well, I didn't see myself as a disruptor.

To me, 'disruptive' people were the high profile movers and shakers, the game changers, and the innovators that hit the news headlines. They were making a big noise in the city. They were loudly and confrontationally challenging anything and everything, with a vision to bring about change on a global scale, and it just didn't feel like me.

At school, the disruptive ones were the ones causing trouble and being a general pain in the butt for teachers and fellow students alike. They were the ones getting in the way of everyone else,. the ones drawing attention to themselves and making a fuss in a 'look at me! Look at me!' way, and I didn't (and don't) want to be like them.

So often, though, we limit our definitions and therefore exclude ourselves from a place at the table. Being a disruptor does not have to mean turning into a raving extrovert, marching to the top of the hill, and, amid fanfare and shouts, planting our flag noisily at the top.

One of my favourite quotes is from H. Jackson Brown: "In the confrontation between the rock and the stream, the stream always wins – not through strength but by perseverance." For me, though, it's like this: disruption is that rock, standing firm in itself and changing the course of the river and, ultimately, the shape of the valley. Disruption can start with a quiet 'excuse me' and a subtle determination to go our own way in the face of societal pressures and other people's opinions in order to bring about lasting change–change that might not be blazing a trail like a bolt of lightning so much as consistently lighting candle after candle after candle, and ultimately flooding the room with lasting light.

It turns out that I come from a long line of disruptors. My great grandmother, Hira, was born in northern India in the late 1800s. At a pivotal point in her young life, the region where she lived was struck by severe famine. With the loss of family and friends around her and facing the possibility of starvation herself, she and her sister - both in their later teens – decided to leave and head south. Whether or not they had a clear plan or knew where they were going is anybody's guess: they just knew that their best chance of survival was in gathering what meagre belongings they could carry, leaving everything they knew, and heading off into the unknown.

Somewhere on the journey, they were approached by a group of people. My great grandmother's sister, exhausted, traumatized by their ordeal, and fearing the worst, panicked and ran off into the jungle. She was never seen or heard of again, and although my great grandmother never stopped looking for her, no trace of her was ever found. Had she stayed, she would have survived; the approaching group were missionaries, who took Hira in. In a new town in a different state far from home, with different customs and languages, she put down roots with the support of her new community. She converted to Christianity, married, and had a family of her own.

Hira's daughter Martha was my grandmother. Following in Indian traditions of the time, she was introduced to and married a man from a nearby town and moved there to be with him. Here, a family mystery creeps in: some say my grandfather died soon after his third daughter was born. A darker family story says that he succumbed to alcoholism and made life impossibly difficult for my grandmother and her children. Either way, her brothers brought her back to her hometown, and with their support, she lived as a single mother and raised three daughters. In many countries in the 1930s and 40s, this was not the norm – in India, it was pretty much unthinkable.

My mother, Madhukanta (or Honey, as it translates in English), grew up in that single-parent family in India with two sisters. Career choices for women were limited then – you'd either become a teacher or a nurse and when you got married, you'd give it all up to be a full-time wife and mother. She had always wanted to be a doctor, but with that choice not open to her, she studied nursing instead as the next best thing.

She studied hard and was determined to go as far as she could: early in her career, she was spotted as a 'rising star,' and at one point she was offered a role on the private medical team of the Maharaja of Baroda. To the astonishment of her tutors and supervisors, she turned it down; for her, the future lay not in the palaces of royalty, but in further training in London, a place she had never visited but only read about.

In the early 1960s, my mother became the first of her family to leave India to study overseas and continued her nursing career in the UK. Again she excelled, and at the height of her career, she was the theatre sister to one of the world's top eye surgeons, working in London's prestigious Harley Street. When she met my dad and became engaged, her family in India gave her two weeks to pack her bags and go home, but she didn't. She married and had two children… and this is where my own story comes in.

My own 'disruption' probably started early on. I was one of those annoying kids who was always asking 'why' – not because I was trying to be a nuisance, but because I genuinely wanted to know. I remember being taken aside by my English teacher once, and being told that I was 'too forthright.' I hadn't been playing up in class (I was quite studious and tended to get good grades), I was just a bit too direct with my opinions, and with my questions as to 'why.'

The same level of directness and questioning landed me in trouble more than once in the workplace, where challenging 'the way things are' led me to be called up in front of the boss, and in one instance, fired.

For the past 20 years, though, asking 'why' and finding answers to that question is one of the factors that has brought me client after client and taken me all over the world.

Why? Because that perennial question of 'why are we doing it like this?' lies at the root of pretty much all business problems. The answer takes us away from a helpless 'well…just because' to a real exploration of cause and a route toward solutions.

One of the things about being a disruptor is that they don't necessarily set out to be disruptive. They aren't deliberately doing the old 'when everyone else zigs, ZAG!' thing just to be contentious, polarizing, or different. They simply have a purpose, a cause, or an idea that they stand for and will not be moved away from. To other people who are challenged by that, it's disruptive, it's different, and it's probably a bit inconvenient simply because it's not the same old same old.

I believe any of us - all of us - can be disruptive and make a bigger impact than we think we can, and it starts with these five factors:

1) Questioning

I was sitting in a hotel room in Cincinnati, having just delivered a leadership training programme to a corporate client. It had been a great course with enthusiastic, receptive participants, but for some reason, I felt really flat.

Looking out of the window that cold winter's day, I started to ask 'why.' Why was I feeling flat? Why did the training I had just delivered feel a bit 'same old same old?' Why did I feel that there must be a better way?

My answers led to the writing of my Amazon Bestseller *Get Your Peas In A Row – 5 key factors to propel your business forward*, in which I set out a framework for sustainable business growth based on five principles of personal development, purpose, people, process, and paradigms.

I had recognized in that 'Cincinnati moment' that growing leaders and businesses is NOT a matter of picking off various business skills topic by topic in the traditional 'training course' way. It's systemic. A business is an ecosystem with co-dependencies at every level. There is no 'silver bullet' to fix the problem – it HAS to be addressed holistically. For me (and later my clients), this was a game changer.

If you've ever wondered "Why are we doing it like this? Why can't we….?. Why do we have to….?" then you've already taken the first step towards becoming a disruptor: querying the status quo and finding your own way forward.

2) Non-Acceptance of Traditional Answers

It can be easy enough to ask the 'why' question, but what's your response to the answer you get? Often we'll get a 'because that's the way it is' type answer, to which many – if not most– will reply "Oh, okay," and carry on as they are.

The disruptor, though, thinks: "Hmm. Not sure if I buy that," and continues to ask questions and look for alternatives. And once they have, decisions have to be made: to play safe and do what everyone else is doing, or to stick your neck out and try something new?

For my great grandmother fleeing famine, my grandmother bringing up three girls as a single parent, and my mother leaving India to further her training overseas, the 'traditional' way forward was what they questioned, and then they chose their own way forward.

Earlier on in my career, when I was in my 20s, I set up a major contract with a large new client for my employer. At the start of the sales process, I'd just picked up the phone and asked to speak to a particular person in senior management. The colleague I shared an office with was aghast: "You can't just pick up the phone and ask to speak to the director!" he exclaimed.

"Why not?" I replied. I wasn't being brave or outrageous. It just hadn't occurred to me that calling a senior executive at a prospective client company was something I shouldn't do.

"It's… it's just not what you do!" he spluttered.

He was older than me and had more experience, and in normal circumstances, I'd have taken his advice and followed protocol. On this occasion, though, I just thought 'why the heck not?!' and – probably more out of annoyance at his butting in and stubbornness on my part – I made the call anyway.

The long and short of it was that following that call and a lengthy procurement process, we won the contract – one of the biggest our company had undertaken at that time.

If I'd accepted his answer, we probably wouldn't have.

3) Standing in the Storm

In the short term, disruptors can often find themselves on the wrong side of the popularity divide simply because they are not following the crowd. It can be unsettling. You can feel isolated and alone, impostor syndrome can creep up on you, and at its worst all of this can lead you to think that you've got it wrong or that it'd be easier just to backtrack and follow the crowd again where there's safety in numbers.

It's at times like these when character and resilience are built.

Years ago, when I advocated experiential rather than classroom-based learning to my clients, my ideas were often dismissed as not 'serious' enough, or just 'a bit of fun' and an unnecessary expense. At times, I was genuinely concerned that maybe I HAD got it wrong, maybe what people wanted WAS a textbook-based, more academic approach to business training. Maybe I WAS being frivolous. Now though, the value of taking time out of the office or workplace environment to think more broadly and learn from the life experiences of others and the lasting psychological impact of experiential learning is well recognized.

If you earnestly believe something to be true, keep saying it until someone listens. When they do, you'll start to notice people rallying to your banner as they recognise that there IS an alternative way forward to the old norms. These people will become your tribe. Weather the storm until you find them.

4) Self Definition

As human beings, we're good at putting people in 'boxes' and applying labels to them. We do it subconsciously to other people, and they most certainly do it to us.

A few years ago, I did some research among women who were extremely successful in their fields: some were company directors and C-suite executives, some were business founders, and others had made their way forward in extremely male-dominated environments, including one who was the overall manager of an oil rig in the North Sea.

One of the many insights to come out of the conversations is that they didn't see themselves as 'women in a male-dominated field' or 'female business owners' or whatever, but just as people getting on with it. As one of them said, "What do you call a female aeronautical engineer? An aeronautical engineer."

Whilst others around them might have tried consciously or subconsciously to define them in some way - to see them as 'women whatevers,' 'boss babes,' 'ballbreakers,' or worse - they just saw themselves as 'me.' They were not overly influenced by what naysayers thought about them.

Now, I do know that there are all too many situations where prejudice exists and it's not that easy. Focusing on what lies beyond the blocker rather than the blocker itself can help, though, in terms of your resilience. As soon as you start to think, 'It's because I'm mixed race' or 'It's because I'm a mother,' you're focusing on the same things they are, rather than on your message and purpose.

I've worked in many male-dominated industries over the years, and there have been times when those I've worked with expected me to do the typing and make the tea rather than lead the meeting. But that was irrelevant to me because I just thought to myself, 'You don't get to define me. I define me. Someone else can get the tea.'

5) Work on Yourself First

Looking back, I recognise that diplomacy and learning how to influence others are core skills that, in my early career, I simply did not have. I might have felt that I had a right to question, that I had a point to make, and indeed, that I was 'right,' but I can see now that I was a bit of a moron in how I came across at least some of the time.

Question, yes. Challenge, yes. Present alternatives, yes. For me, doing these things with compassion and respect is paramount. Anyone – disruptor or not – who doesn't develop their skills may eventually find themselves irrelevant, however compelling they believe their message to be. We are all works in progress, and ongoing personal development is essential.

So, my sister disruptors and would-be disruptors. Don't underestimate your power or the reach of your influence. Above all, don't let fear cause you to settle for anything less than you deserve.

Question your world. Make bold, game-changing choices. Find your voice. Bring others with you. In doing so, you can and will change the world.

Heather Stokes Benton

CEO/Owner/Founder of Financial GPS

https://www.linkedin.com/in/heather-stokes-benton-wealth-navigator-899624204/
https://www.facebook.com/heather.benton.1675
https://www.facebook.com/financiallyfocusedfamilies
https://www.facebook.com/groups/490021218981192
https://www.instagram.com/heathersfinancialfocus/
https://open.spotify.com/show/7hb8W1oPbkv4UrgUz1ws9O?si=a459cd08ac3f4b73

I am a wife, mother, homeschooler, and business owner. I am a giver, a motivator, a developer, and I do not accept the answer no. I only see it as a challenge. My road to success has changed many times. Life has derailed my journey and I have built a new path each time. I went to college for Forensic Psychology and worked for multiple government agencies over the next eight years. When I met my husband he was a flight attendant and owned a limousine business. We lived a lavish life. 9/11 was our first major setback, three years later he suffered a major injury and then pancreatic cancer at 40. I could have given up, but with three girls depending on us that was not an option. I had to learn how to be creative with money. Now it is my mission to help others to go from surviving to thriving. Being a mother and running a business can feel overwhelming at times. I find the key to keeping it all together is balance.

DISRUPTING WITH GRACE

By Heather Stokes Benton

I grew up more of an observer. My mother has always been independent and a hard worker. My father had a political role with the sheriff's office and both were educated. They instilled in us hard work, respectfulness, and diplomacy. I grew up knowing my duty and my role but also with a voice. We were encouraged to speak our peace and involved in adult conversations. We were taught to think before speaking, but that our opinions were valued even if we did not all agree. I have never been one to easily accept the word no. I viewed it more as a challenge, and I never shy away from a challenge. I see it as an opportunity to prove them wrong. Can't afford it? Make more money. It's not for you? Watch me. Don't want me to sit at your table? No worries, I will build my own damn table.

I remember in my high school and college years my parents paid for the basics and classes, because they did not want me struggling like them or dividing my time with studies. But I wanted more. So, if I wanted more than what they were able to provide, I did it myself. From babysitting to side jobs and car rides, I was uber before it even existed. Later, when I was ready to move out even though they said no, I worked several jobs in addition to a full course load in college. I remember working the graveyard shift until 7 AM then sleeping in the car for two hours and going to class at 9 AM. I would catch a cat nap later in the afternoon and head back to work again. Somehow I still found time for friends, family, and fun. I graduated with a degree in Psychology and a double minor in Criminology and Forensics.

My first job was with the in-jail drug program. I started there as an intern, unpaid mind you, while working three jobs and finishing school. After two years, I helped start a pilot program for mental health and forensic psychology in the jail system helping mentally ill, non-violent offenders get back on medication and in support programs. I sat on committees and in courtrooms with judges and county leaders. At times it was mind-blowing that these accomplished leaders 2-3 times my senior were even listening to my recommendations on how to best serve the population. In reality, they were more mind blown by my knowledge, composure, and ability. Several times a week I was butting heads with judges, and 90% of the time I won as long as I had done my research and could give them facts and stats they could not argue against. Most of the attorneys just sat down and let me take the floor.

But it was not all sunshine and roses. After about five years, I wanted a change. I took on a new position with the sheriff's office in the child protection division. I helped families during challenging situations. Of course, there were sad days when I had to remove children for their safety. I like helping families improve their lives, but I quickly learned I was not cut out for bureaucracy and politics. Let's just say they like to take orders and not ask questions, and that is just not me. When I became pregnant with my first child, I left knowing I did not want to be pregnant in that environment.

I had no idea what was coming, but my life of serving the community and others was about to change. Seven years prior, I met my husband. When we first met he was a flight attendant with Delta Airlines and owned a limousine service. The idea of being a business owner was new to me. I quickly learned the benefits and challenges of being a business owner. For a while, we were on top of the world, flying places on a whim and traveling in style. Our business was growing, and our professional careers were on an upward track. 9/11 was our first major setback. He was furloughed for a year, and we had to restructure because, like most of those affected, the bills keep coming. Thankfully we still had the business, but people were not renting limos as much as before. We downsized and sold annual packages to survive. About a year later, he was brought back full-time when life threw us another curveball. He suffered a major injury inflight and was placed on leave. Nine surgeries and six months of physical therapy later, he still physically could not return. After 10 years he had to say goodbye to his career with Delta. It was a crippling blow for our family, especially since we had just taken full custody of his then 10-year-old daughter.

I tell you all this because even when we stand up for ourselves and others, life will still slap us sideways and we have to rebuild, redesign, and not take no for an answer. Just when I thought I had seen and survived it all, life slapped us in the face and showed me I hadn't seen anything yet. My stepdaughter was 14 and my daughter was 18 months old when my husband was diagnosed with a large pancreatic mass and told he had less than three months to live unless he had it surgically removed, and there was no guarantee. We had a few short weeks to get our affairs in order and prepare for the worst. We spent a small fortune filing legal paperwork just in case he didn't survive. We had very hard conversations I never imagined having with my husband, who was only 40 years old at the time. He survived the six hour surgery, but physically, medically, and emotionally, he changed. It was a long eight months of recovery. Amazingly, it's been almost 10 years.

It's been a hard road, and he has had some major medical setbacks. We had to close the business and sell cars and assets, and we lived off those for several years. God blessed us with another daughter. We downsized and restructured again. These hard years taught me unconditional love, faith, and perseverance. It was what I experienced there that would later push me into entrepreneurship, homeschooling my children, and taught me humility.

I enjoy being a wife, a mother, homeschooler, cooking, baking, and making memories every day. We have lived with the fear of losing him for so long that we were simply existing in survival mode. I got lost in surviving and I forgot about thriving. I couldn't just give up with three girls depending on me. I set out on a mission to change the direction of my life and build a legacy for my children. It was through this refocusing that I found a new mindset, new goals, and the peace of mind I had missed for years.

I did my research and decided to open a financial services business that would educate and help others to be prepared for these types of life sideswipes. We all should know how to make money, grow money, save money, be prepared, and change our family's generational story. I was told I was crazy, people don't talk about money that way, you need years to build clientele, and money is still a man's world. Even as I build my business, I got the cold shoulder or was told that is not the way to do it. I decided it was time to build my own damn table.

In 2020, like most of us, I was pushed out of my comfort zone. I had just started my journey to Financial Freedom, my solo business, and the pandemic slapped me right in the face. I had been through so much already, and I was not about to let this get me down. I had little to no social media, and now for my company to survive, I was going to have to adjust to online promotions and living in Zoom land. As I had often been told, growth is uncomfortable. Mainly because it is something you have never done before. I found I had to embrace it and give myself grace. In the beginning, I didn't want to post unless it was perfect. I looked for approval constantly. I was worried about what my family and friends would think about me talking business online.

I realized I was a voice that needed to be heard. It didn't have to be perfect, it just needed to be shared. Money is hard to talk about, and many will shy away from it, but that is our problem. We need hard conversations. Sometimes we need the slap in the face, and if I am talking and posting about how to better yourself financially through growth and development, then you are probably hiding from your own money demons.

I find people keep waiting for things to be right financially, but don't take the action they need to change their financial direction. Whether you do it or not, life will not be the same a year from now, five years from now, and 10 years from now. Make the decisions at this moment that will lead you towards the future you want.

I decided in 2021 to change the name of my business to Financial GPS, because we don't plan to fail, we fail to plan. I wanted to be a beacon of hope for women and families to plan for a better future, and there are so many vehicles to do that with. Then later in 2021, I started guest speaking to further educate others to take action to change their money mindset from surviving to thriving. Before I knew it I was co-authoring books and running my own podcast. I would have never guessed even five years ago that I would be a voice for others' financial freedom, that I would be here writing in my sixth book now, and helping women all over the world to step up and step out. Don't listen to the noise, the naysayers, and the excuse makers, just be you. Be the difference. You don't have to push others down to do it. You can do it with grace. Just step out of your comfort zone, don't settle, and show everyone a different way.

The craziest part of the whole journey has been the impact I unknowingly had on my girls. While writing my second book, they came to me and asked if they could write a book and publish it too, like me. I paused at the request, mainly in shock. My middle daughter responded, "We figured if you can do it, we can do it too." My response was, "Of course you can." She and her sister, only six at the time, worked together writing and illustrating a children's book. Most parents would have laughed, said maybe when you are older, or the kids would have started and never finished. However, I saw this as an opportunity for them to rise up and do something out of the ordinary for their age.

The six year old became the youngest international bestseller, and her older sister just released her first solo book at the beginning of this year, hitting best seller in four countries and 12 categories. I tell you this not just to brag about my kids but to show you that you can do anything you put your mind to. If they can do it, you can too. Be the change, be the difference, step out, and step up. The world is watching and they want to hear your voice.

I have held several other leadership roles not even mentioned in this chapter, but on more than one occasion I have been told that I lead with grace. I take this as a compliment. It's not grace as in meek or weak, it's that I do not let others bring me down or phase me. When someone says no or I can't, I don't question or yell. I just work around them, replace them, show them how it is done, or make a new path. Life is too short to settle, give up, or give into failure or loss. It's perseverance that defines you.

"Those who disrupt their industries change consumer behavior, alter economics, and transform lives."
—Heather Simmons

JOIN THE MOVEMENT!
#BAUW

Becoming An Unstoppable Woman
With She Rises Studios

She Rises Studios was founded by Hanna Olivas and Adriana Luna Carlos, the mother-daughter duo, in mid-2020 as they saw a need to help empower women around the world. They are the podcast hosts of the *She Rises Studios Podcast* as well as Amazon best-selling authors and motivational speakers who travel the world. Hanna and Adriana are the movement creators of #BAUW - Becoming An Unstoppable Woman: The movement has been created to universally impact women of all ages, at whatever stage of life, to overcome insecurities, and adversities, and develop an unstoppable mindset. She Rises Studios educates, celebrates, and empowers women globally.

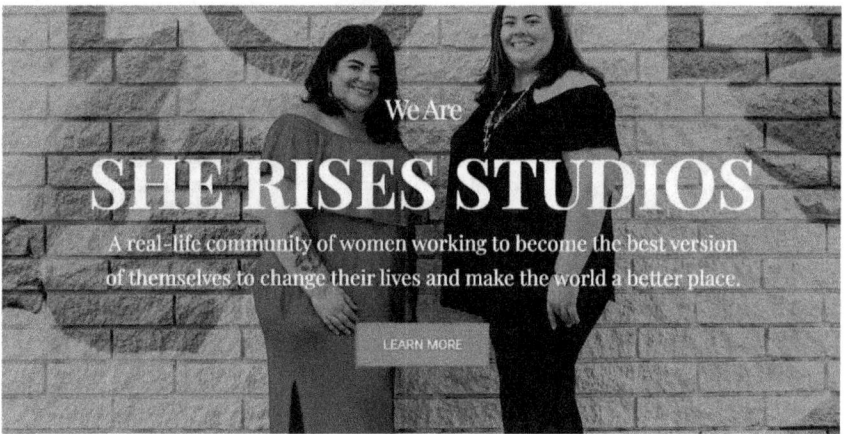

Looking to Join Us in our Next Anthology or Publish YOUR Own?

She Rises Studios Publishing offers full-service publishing, marketing, book tour, and campaign services. For more information, contact info@sherisesstudios.com

We are always looking for women who want to share their stories and expertise and feature their businesses on our podcasts, in our books, and in our magazines.

SEE WHAT WE DO

OUR PODCAST

OUR BOOKS

OUR SERVICES

Be featured in the Becoming An Unstoppable Woman magazine, published in 13 countries and sold in all major retailers. Get the visibility you need to LEVEL UP in your business!

Have your own TV show streamed across major platforms like Roku TV, Amazon Fire Stick, Apple TV and more!

Learn to leverage your expertise. Build your online presence and grow your audience with Fenix TV.
https://fenixtv.sherisesstudios.com/

Visit www.SheRisesStudios.com to see how YOU can join the #BAUW movement and help your community to achieve the UNSTOPPABLE mindset.

Have you checked out the *She Rises Studios Podcast?*

Find us on all MAJOR platforms: Spotify, IHeartRadio, Apple Podcasts, Google Podcasts, etc.

Looking to become a sponsor or build a partnership?

Email us at info@sherisesstudios.com

SHE RISES
S T U D I O S